The

GROWING & MANAGING A BUSINESS
25 KEYS TO BUILDING YOUR COMPANY

KATHLEEN R. ALLEN, PH.D.
Marshall School of Business
University of Southern California

Lebhar-Friedman Books
NEW YORK • CHICAGO • LOS ANGELES • LONDON • PARIS • TOKYO

For *The New York Times*
Mike Levitas, Editorial Director, Book Development
Tom Redburn, General Series Editor
Brent Bowers, Series Editor
James Schembari, Series Editor

Lebhar-Friedman Books
425 Park Avenue
New York, NY 10022

Copyright © 1999 *The New York Times*

Published by Lebhar-Friedman Books
Lebhar-Friedman Books is a company of Lebhar-Friedman Inc.

Printed in the United States of America

Library of Congress Cataloging-in-Publication Data
Allen, Kathleen R.
    Growing & managing a business : 25 keys to building your
company / Kathleen R. Allen.
       p.   cm.—(The New York Times pocket MBA series ; v. 4)
    Includes index.
    ISBN 0-86730-774-9 (pbk.)
    1. Management.   2. Entrepreneurship.   3. Success in business.
I. Title. II. Title: Growing and managing a business.   III. Series.
    HD31.A412   1999
    658—dc21   99-37755
                                                                        CIP

DESIGN & PRODUCTION BY MILLER WILLIAMS DESIGN ASSOCIATES

Visit our Web site at lfbooks.com

INTRODUCTION

LEBHAR-FRIEDMAN BOOKS is proud to present *The New York Times* Pocket MBA Series, 12 invaluable reference volumes that are easily accessible to all businesspersons, from first level managers to the executive suite. The books are written by Ph.D.s who teach in the MBA programs in some of the finest schools in the country. A team of business editors from *The New York Times*— Mike Levitas, Tom Redburn, Brent Bowers, and James Schembari—provided their own expertise to edit a reference series that is beyond compare.

The New York Times Pocket MBA Series offers quick-reference key points learned in top MBA programs. The 25-key structure of each volume presents an unparalleled synopsis of crucial principles of specific areas of business expertise. The unique approach to this series packages academic books for consumers in an easy-to-use trade format that is ideal for the individual businessperson as well as an excellent training reference manual. Be sure to get all 12 titles in the series to complete your own MBA education.

Joseph Mills
Senior Managing Editor
Lebhar-Friedman Books

The New York Times Pocket MBA
Series includes these 12 volumes:

Analyzing Financial Statements

Business Planning

Business Financing

Growing & Managing a Business

Organizing a Company

Forecasting Budgets

Tracking & Controlling Costs

Sales & Marketing

Managing Investment

Going Global

Leadership & Vision

The Board of Directors

25 KEYS TO BUILDING YOUR COMPANY

CONTENTS

KEY 1

Prepare yourself and your company for growth

I f you have survived the trauma of birth and successfully started a company, the natural byproduct will be growth. Most people think of birth and the very early stages in the life of a business as the most dangerous time. The reality, however, is that the growth stage is likely to be even more perilous, because growth often catches the entrepreneur unaware and unprepared. How can this possibly happen?

The start-up stage of a company is a demanding time for entrepreneurs. They are so busy making everything happen that there is rarely time to scan the horizon to see what's coming. Consequently, entrepreneurs often do not realize that once the business reaches critical mass in terms of customer awareness, demand usually increases dramatically. That translates into immediate needs for the business and the entrepreneur.

Entrepreneurs are considered by many as "control freaks." Because the business results from their financial and sweat equity, they are naturally reluctant to delegate responsibility to others. They believe that no one can do what they do better than they can. That simply is not true. The skills required to create an opportunity and assemble the resources to start the business are not the same skills necessary to grow the business. Growing the business requires professional management skills, and typically the entrepreneur will have to bring someone on board who has the skills that he lacks.

At a minimum, you will benefit from establishing an advisory board of experienced business people who can guide you through the growth process. It is likely, however, that you will also need to hire people to set up the strategies, controls, and systems for growth. Greg Levin, who started the Boston-based company PerfectCurve® with his father, recognized that. The company manufactures and distributes baseball cap accessories to more than 350 retail outlets and catalogs around the country. The company is most known for its PerfectCurve, a simple device that creates a curved cap brim on baseball caps. As the product gained acceptance and demand exploded, Levin made sure that he surrounded himself with people who knew more than he did about how to grow this type of business, and he attributes his company's success to that decision.

Just as a business plan was a critical component in starting a company, a growth plan is vital to its expansion. This should include your overall growth strategy, the specific tactics you will use to execute that strategy, and the resources that will be required to undertake those tactics. Those resources usually include additional staffing to meet the increased workload, standardized systems or procedures for how things should be done, and controls to provide benchmarks and checkpoints for monitoring the company during growth. The plan should also specify how you plan to secure working capital and financing for any new equipment and facilities.

In the following keys, you will learn the methods of successful growth for any business.

He who thinks his business below him, will always be above his business.

Thomas Fuller, **Gnomologia**

KEY 2

Be aware of the factors that affect your company's ability to grow

Growing your business is a little like going into battle. It is important to know your enemy. If you don't understand all the obstacles to growth, you won't be prepared to deal with them. Douglas Levin certainly learned that lesson the hard way. He started by paying too much for his fresh juice company, Fresh Samantha, he says. That meant he had less room for error in the decisions he would make. Then he mistakenly targeted the wrong market, so consumers thought the price of his juices was too high. And if that weren't enough, a competitor sold a batch of apple juice that contained the *E. Coli* bacteria, and Levin, like other juice manufacturers, had to invest in expensive pasteurization equipment. All of these problems halted his growth for a time, and it was only his persistence that finally allowed the company to grow from $2.8 million in 1996 to $7 million in 1997.

Several factors can affect your ability to grow your company.

Your intentions. Some entrepreneurs actually choose not to grow or to grow very slowly. This reluctance is usually out of fear. It's important to understand that you have to want to grow your business or you will not do what is necessary to make it happen.

The nature of your target market. The size of your market and its buying power will certainly put limits on how much and how fast you can grow. You can expand those limits by looking at global markets or adding more products and services to your offerings.

The nature of your competition. You choose your competition based on how you define the market niche you are entering. If you intend to go head to head with a much larger, more established company, you are asking for trouble. You would be better off creating a customer niche that is currently not served by the larger companies in the market to give your company a chance to gain a foothold before it takes on larger competitors.

How your industry deals with innovation. If you are fortunate enough to be in an industry where innovation is rare, you can gain a competitive advantage by introducing something new—a new product or a new way of doing something. If, on the other hand, you find yourself in an industry where innovation is the price of admission, you will need significant capital resources to survive.

How predictable your industry is. Predictability certainly makes business life easier, but the truth is, it makes it so much easier that it is difficult to differentiate yourself and do well in the market. By contrast, a highly volatile industry like telecommunications can be a hotbed of opportunity because things are changing so rapidly. Small companies can often benefit the most because they tend to be more flexible with much lower overhead, and they can change course quickly as needed.

How difficult entry barriers are. Your industry is not always a friendly place. Mature players can make it very difficult for new businesses to enter by setting high standards for research and development, plant and equipment, or regulations. Established businesses that own core technology can effectively keep you from playing by refusing to license that technology.

Knowing the factors that could prevent you from achieving your goals will give you a chance to find ways to successfully deal with them before you reach the growth stage.

KEY 3

To grow, your company needs a vision

There is an old saying, "If you don't where you're going, how will you know when you've gotten there?" That certainly holds true for growing businesses. Superstar athletes like Michael Jordan visualize games before they play them. Successful entrepreneurs also envision where they want their companies to be in the future.

Vision is the glue that holds everyone in the company together in a common purpose. The research of people like Jim Collins and Jerry Porras[1] has taught us that a company can be profitable without a vision, but vision appears to be essential for a company to endure over time. Vision provides the environment conducive to making the right decisions.

The problem is that most entrepreneurs get so wrapped up in the day-to-day activities of

---

[1]Collins, Jim and Jerry I. Porras (1994). *Built to Last, Successful Habits of Visionary Companies*, New York: Harper Business, 1994.

keeping the business moving forward that they rarely raise their heads above the fray to see what's coming. Moreover, they have no idea where they are going. This is a critical mistake. Defining where you want the business to be at some point in the future allows you to make better decisions along the way. In other words, you will make decisions that take your business in the right direction.

The foundation of any business's vision is the value system of the entrepreneur. Collins and Porras called this "core values," and they represent your fundamental philosophy of life, what you believe in. Core values are long-held beliefs and are unlikely to change. If you are willing to change a belief you have, then it is probably not a core value. Here are some examples of core values that some business owners have expressed:

We believe in total integrity.

Our employees are our most important asset.

We will treat everyone fairly and honestly.

The core values you define for your business are sacred. You would never do anything to compromise those values because they are the values by which your company is known. For example, if your employees are your most important asset, you would never treat them like mere cogs who have no say in what happens. Rather, you would treat them like members of the team, who have a vested interest in the success of the business.

It follows that you should involve your employees in the definition of the other core values for your business. That will be easier if your business is new because you will probably hire people who have the same core values you do. If, on the other hand, you have an existing business, you will need to get your employees to "buy in" to the values you want to your business to espouse.

If you build a vision for your company that is based on your core values, it is more likely that you will achieve that vision.

Humans must breathe,

but corporations must

make money.

Alice Embree, **Sisterhood Is Powerful**

KEY 4

Put systems and controls in place to manage growth effectively

---

One of the primary reasons many businesses experience problems during rapid growth is that they have failed to put in place effective systems and controls—policies and procedures for doing things, and checks and balances to make sure the company is on target. Without these, the company runs out of control. The purpose of systems and controls is to manage organizational activities so that the company can achieve its expected performance level while it continues to grow.

Today, more than ever before, it's important for businesses to have procedures and benchmarks against which to judge their progress. The environment in which most businesses operate is dynamic, constantly changing. Suppose your business has set a standard of 100 percent on-time delivery of its products. If you don't have a system in place to keeping track of deliveries and check on your performance, how will you know whether you are meeting it?

Or suppose that you have established a quality standard for your product, and even so one of your biggest customers suddenly stops ordering from you on the grounds that the product is substandard. What happened? What happened is that while you were busy running your business, you didn't notice that your competitors had raised the quality bar. What used to be high quality is now substandard. Change can happen that quickly. Having systems in place to check on market conditions and, especially, your competitors' actions, will help prevent such rude surprises.

Having systems in place will also help you manage a complex organization much more easily. Entrepreneurs often overlook the fact that an error in one area of the company has an impact throughout the organization, and that can be very costly, even potentially devastating to the company. Emery Worldwide, the air freight company, was a very profitable company until it purchased Purolator Courier Corporation in 1987, adding to the complexity of its organization. Emery was unprepared to manage such a large company and had no systems in place to do so. Consequently, it began losing money, its costs increased, its service declined, and the company nearly went bankrupt. It was only through the creation of systems and controls that the company survived and began a turnaround. It was ultimately purchased by Consolidated Freightways Inc.

There are four basic types of systems and controls. Physical controls include inventory management, quality control, and equipment management. You should maintain as small an inventory as you can and still provide customers what they want when they want it. You will also want to constantly improve the quality of everything your company does and make sure you have the necessary equipment and facilities in place when you need them.

Control of your human resources includes good systems for hiring, retaining, and dismissing employees, as well as training and development of employees. Controlling information resources is about managing the information you need to be competitive in the marketplace, such as sales forecasts, market analyses, and production scheduling. Finally, financial controls affect every area of the organization. Systems for managing the cash flow of the company, timing purchases correctly, and managing accounts receivable effectively are just some of the types of financial controls you will need. A good control system will establish standards, measure performance, compare performance against the standards, and then provide for a way to correct procedures where needed.

KEY 5

Develop a strong, professional management team

A business can run for quite some time on the strength and expertise of the founders. But the skills and abilities that created the company and saw it through the critical start-up stage are not the skills and abilities required to grow the business to the next level. When a business has reached the point where it is poised to grow from a small business to a mid-sized business or from a mid-sized business to a large business, it needs professional management skills that most entrepreneurs don't possess and, frankly, have no desire to possess.

Rapid growth puts new and often life-threatening stresses and strains on the business. If effective systems and controls are not in place, growth can veer out of control and actually hurt the company. The people who can help the business manage its growth competently are professionals with experience in the core functions of the business: finance, marketing, and operations. They will also be able to put in

To business that we love
we rise at bedtime, and
go to with delight.

Shakespeare, Antony and Cleopatra

place the structure and systems that will allow the business to compete on a more level playing field with much larger companies. They will be able to advise the owners on sound strategies to manage increasing demand.

The question of when to bring on professional management is a perplexing one. The new high-tech, high-growth Internet companies that can go through "hockey stick" growth (so named because the line charting it often looks like a hockey stick) and do an initial public offering in less than 12 months often start with professional management, because there isn't time to bring people on board in the midst of hyperactivity.

The chief executives of most other types of companies, on the other hand, have time to sense when their businesses are about to reach critical mass and shift into rapid growth. Critical mass is different for every company, but it is usually measured by the number of customers it takes to create enough awareness in the marketplace for the business to take off. The trick is to recognize the approach of critical mass in time to prepare for the onset of rapid growth.

To be sure, bringing professional management into an entrepreneurial business can have its downside. Steve Rifkind found that to be true when he hired a movie-company executive to head the movie division of his music and clothing business that targets urban youth. Mr. Rifkind thought that the movie mogul would fit right into the lean-and-mean entrepreneurial culture he had created. He could not have been more wrong. Accustomed to a big staff and expensive office space, the new executive increased expenditures enormously without increasing revenues at all. In all, Rifkind lost $5 million on a poor choice and went back to where he started, a bit shell-shocked but a whole lot wiser.[2]

The important lesson is that in addition to finding professional management that has the skills you need, you also have to find people who share the company's core values and aren't trying to bring the mega-corporate model to a scrappy, mid-sized company. It is entirely possible to grow and maintain the entrepreneurial spirit as your business becomes more professional, but it requires finding the right people with the right attitude.

[2]Susan Greco, "Share the Power," *Inc.*, February, 1999, p. 52.

KEY 6

Find your competitive advantage and sustain it

If someone asked you to state in one sentence your business's competitive advantage, could you do it? If I sat across the table from you and asked you to tell me in a single sentence why I should buy from you rather than your competitor, could you do it? You might be saying, "Of course, my competitive advantage is customer service," or "Absolutely, my advantage is quality." Would it surprise you to learn that you'd be wrong on both counts? I'm not saying that customer service and quality aren't important—they are very important. They just aren't what gives your business a competitive advantage in the marketplace over and above other businesses that also claim these two advantages.

Your competitive advantage is what distinguishes your business from all others in the markets in which you compete. It may not have anything to do with your product or service quality. For Northwest Airlines, their raucous, fun-loving company culture sets them apart. They make flying fun. Brian Robinson was able to successfully compete against giant Price/Costco in the warehouse products market by giving customers the ability to buy at warehouse prices without having to buy in bulk and with no membership fees. His key to success was finding out what the "big boys" weren't doing, and then doing it well himself.

To find your competitive advantage, you need to know your industry. Every industry, no matter how difficult, offers countless opportunities for small companies to create a competitive advantage. Begin by looking carefully at your business. Have you planned for the resources and capabilities you will need to take advantage of any opportunities that come along? Industry environments are very dynamic today, so business owners have to be constantly scanning the horizon for changes that can afford them an opportunity to gain an advantage.

Does your company have any competencies or resources that are rare in the industry? After all, if everyone shares the same competencies or resources, then no one has a competitive advantage. That's why some restaurants have attached themselves to celebrities to gain an edge that other restaurants don't have.

Do you have management control systems, a formal reporting structure, or a technology that will help you acquire and process information better than your competitors? These may not be as sexy as a movie star's endorsement, but managing growth well is a competitive advantage that many small businesses just don't have. The issue of using technology as a competitive advantage will be dealt with in Key 12, but suffice it to say that for at least the next five years, using technology to improve the processes of your business will be a significant competitive advantage.

To sustain your competitive advantage over the long term, you will need to check constantly not only the opportunities and threats in your environment, but also the resources and capabilities of your company to meet them. You must prepare your business for change as a way of life. Flexibility can be a significant competitive advantage.

KEY 7

Choose the right growth strategy for your business

There are four basic growth strategies—and choosing the right one can mean the difference between prosperity and failure. Here we will provide a brief overview of the four strategies; in later Keys, we will highlight several versions that let a small business grow strategically in healthy ways. The four growth strategies are:

1 Growing within the current market

2 Growing within the industry

3 Growing outside the industry

4 Growing globally

Growing within the current market means, simply, attempting to capture more customers within the market that a business serves. For example, if you sell lamps in Atlanta, you will try to sell even more lamps before moving to another area. This is called market penetration, and is the classic approach of startups. You may grow geographically as well, through a variety of strategies, such as licensing your product or franchising your operations to businesses in other parts of the country. You may also exploit the current market by developing new products and services to sell to current customers. Indeed, selling more to current customers is more cost effective than finding new customers.

Growing within the industry takes you beyond your current customer base by moving vertically or horizontally within the industry. With a vertical integration strategy, you may acquire one of your suppliers and become your own supplier. This will let you provide these goods and services to your own company and other companies as well. Alternatively, you may want to control the distribution of your products horizontally by either selling direct to the customer through a retail outlet, catalogue, sales, or Internet sales or by acquiring one of your distributors.

Yet another way to grow within the industry is to purchase your competitors or a complementary business that provides a new market. For example, if you owned a restaurant, you might purchase a catering company. Now you would have access to corporate customers and organizations that use catering services.

Growing outside the industry is a strategy that involves investing in or acquiring products or businesses outside your business's core competencies. Typically, this strategy is employed when all the others have been exhausted, but not always. Suppose you find that you and your employees are traveling constantly to meet with customers and strategic partners. You might want to consider acquiring a travel company, both to save money and to serve your needs better. You wouldn't be the first entrepreneur to do this; others have purchased businesses that can use the excess capacity they have in their manufacturing facilities.

Growing globally is a way to break out of a saturated market. By looking to global markets, you may find new customers and new applications for your products that may even increase their sales domestically. Look at Key 19 for some hints on global strategy.

Remember that no matter which strategy you choose, successful growth will only come about when you are giving customers what they need when they need it. That is the most important component of any growth strategy.

The citizen is at his

business before he rises.

George Herbert

KEY 8

Consolidation and network strategies can be a winning combination

When one of the most successful entrepreneurs of our time chooses a business strategy and consistently wins with it, people sit up and take notice. Wayne Huizenga did not invent the consolidation, or "Pac Man," strategy, but he certainly perfected it. He began one garbage truck at a time to build billion-dollar Waste Management, Inc. Then he moved on to use the same strategy with video stores to build the billion-dollar Blockbuster Entertainment Corporation. Now he has determined to change the face of the used car industry with Auto Nation, his third billion-dollar company.

The automobile industry is probably the most famous example of consolidation. In 1898, the industry sported more than 2,000 manufacturers. Today we see just a handful because of consolidation to achieve economies of scale and marketing power. Industry consolidation is more widespread today than ever before.

The way it works is this: the consolidator acquires the best company in a given geographic area in a fragmented industry that is dominated by "mom and pop" businesses. The company being acquired typically is worth between $7 million and $20 million and has a long track record of good management and community relations. The owners are usually offered incentives in the form of cash and stock to help build the new business. They are also charged with the responsibility of finding other small businesses to acquire. Each region becomes a profit center with centralized functions like accounting and purchasing.

A consolidation strategy is not just for mega-entrepreneurs like Mr. Huizenga. Todd Smart, a young entrepreneur who was also willing to work in a non-glamorous industry, founded Absolute Towing and Transporting to tow wrecked cars. He did well and was soon buying other independent towing companies. In 1999, he and a partner founded a company and took it public with the express purpose of consolidating the towing industry.

Since using a consolidation strategy requires the valuation of the businesses being acquired, it is important to use attorneys and other specialists in the area to smooth the way and prevent mistakes.

Another path to fast growth is so-called modular, or network, growth strategies—that is, forming a long-term partnership with another company to perform tasks that are peripheral to your core competencies. For example, if the core function of your business is the design and development of new products, then you might outsource the manufacturing of parts, the assembly, and the marketing and distribution. With this approach, your company can grow more rapidly, keep unit costs down, and turn out new products more quickly. You will also not have to invest heavily in fixed assets and instead can put that money toward research and development of new products. Many industries like apparel, film, and electronics have used this strategy for years.

KEY 9

Franchising can be an effective way to grow

One of the more effective strategies for growing quickly without incurring all of the costs of growth yourself is franchising. Franchising simply means selling your business's format to other entrepreneurs. You provide a product or service with a proven market, the use of trademarked names, an accounting and financial control system, a marketing plan, and the benefits of volume purchasing and advertising. The franchisees pay for their own facilities and equipment and pay you a franchise fee and a royalty on sales.

Great Harvest Bread Company of Dillon, Montana, determined that franchising was the best way to grow the business rapidly and still give the owners the freedom they wanted to travel and enjoy life. Unlike many franchisers, Great Harvest encourages its franchisees to be individualists with the only caveat being that their bread must come fresh from the oven and only be sliced as it is used.

Drive thy Business, or it will drive thee.

Benjamin Franklin, Autobiography

In franchising, the entrepreneur is basically licensing his business plan to the franchisee. The franchiser must provide training and assistance in starting the business, and marketing and quality control support as the business is operating.

Not every business is suitable for franchising. Look at your business to see if it has the following characteristics:

- ◆ Do you have a successful prototype store with a good reputation?

- ◆ Do you have a registered trademark and a consistent image for your store(s)?

- ◆ Do you sell a product that will do well in different geographic regions?

- ◆ Is your business the kind that can be systematized and replicated easily?

◆ Do you have an operations manual that details all aspects of your business?

◆ Do financial statements show the company is profitable?

If you can answer yes to these questions, you may have the potential to franchise your business. Franchising is not without risk, however. It takes a lot of work to prepare a franchise opportunity. Some say it's almost like starting a new business all over again. For one thing, you will need to set up a system for screening and training potential franchisees. You will incur significant costs for legal, accounting and consulting work and for preparing a well-documented prospectus that spells out the rights, responsibilities, and risks to the franchisees. It is estimated that about 35 percent of franchises go out of business within four years. As a franchiser, you must manage and support your franchisees so that the overall health of your business stays intact. You must continually monitor quality in your franchisees' businesses because they are representing you and the brand name you have built. Today, more than one out of 12 businesses is a franchise and more than 42,000 franchises start up every year. That is a testament to this growth strategy's effectiveness.

KEY 10

Develop a growth-oriented company culture

Who would have thought that the personality and character of your company might determine whether it succeeds? The reality is that company culture contributes enormously to the financial success and well-being of a company. Researchers certainly don't agree on what culture is. Some define it as the outward manifestation of the core values of the founders; therefore, it is constant, unchanging. Others say that culture changes with the attitudes and behaviors of those in the company at the time. Whatever you believe, culture is the company's particular way of doing things, the unique atmosphere created by the people in the company and the way they do their work.

Amy's Ice Cream, a retail outlet based in Austin, Texas, believes in entertaining its customers. Customers will stand in long lines out the door to not only buy the ice cream but to watch the employees break-dancing on the freezers or singing to the customers as they hand out samples.

The company culture is based on the notion that you can have fun while you work. And the culture works; Amy's now has expanded to multiple outlets.

How can you define your company culture? Start by asking yourself some key questions[3]:

- How do you want your employees to work: in teams or individually?

- How will the company deal with change?

- How will the company deal with failure?

- How are decisions made, and who makes the critical ones?

- How is work prioritized?

- How is information shared within and outside the organization?

- Does the company take a long-term or short-term focus on decision-making?

- How does the company ensure employee competence?

- Does the company encourage diversity?

- How are employees treated, and what is their role in the company's vision?

For example, a company that uses teamwork, celebrates change, learns from failure, allows decision making at all levels and shares information freely will be a much different company

---

[3]Adapted from Kathleen R. Allen, *Growing and Managing an Entrepreneurial Business*, Boston: Houghton Mifflin Company, 1999.

from one that rewards individual behavior, avoids change and failure, limits access to information and makes decisions from the top down. Certainly, the first type of company will be more flexible and able to respond better to a rapidly changing environment.

Culture is important because it has a significant impact on your company's performance. A culture where the employees share the values and norms of the business will be much more focused and driven to achieve the company's goals. Closed circuit TV manufacturer Pelco Inc. has a corporate culture that is based on being "fanatically customer driven." You can talk to anyone in the company, from the president to the worker on the assembly line, and within a matter of minutes you will hear the word *customer*. Everyone knows what he or she contributes to the customer of the customer.

Remember, your company's culture is based on the core values you identify and infuse throughout your organization. Everyone has to buy into these values and this culture for it to take hold. When a sound company culture is achieved, successful growth is possible.

KEY 11

Strategic alliances can help you grow more rapidly

Growing a company has to be a team effort and sometimes that team includes other companies in the industry. Many chief executives have found that forming partnerships with companies that have strengths that theirs lacks allows their business to grow more rapidly. These partnerships are called strategic alliances, and can often mean the difference between a company that grows very slowly, or not at all, and a company that expands to a substantial size. Craftsman Customer Metal Fabricators Inc. is a relatively small company based in Illinois. In the late 1980s, its principal customer was Motorola. At that time Motorola had made a decision to reduce the number of its suppliers and to make the remaining ones partners. What this meant to Craftsman was that it would have to share its trade secrets with a giant company that happened to be its customer, or risk losing that customer. Craftsman decided to try the partnership, and to its surprise found that it benefited immensely from the relationship through innovations it borrowed from Motorola and the resulting ability to save money for its customers. In fact, the company grew from $6 million to $30 million in annual revenue over 10 years.[4]

A good strategic partner should have diversified interests so that it can bear the risk of the relationship with a small company. It should also have experience in these types of partnerships and excess capacity to benefit the smaller company.

And that ye study to be quiet, and to do your own business.

New Testament, 1 Thessalonians

Strategic alliances have many advantages. Because you are outsourcing some of your needs to other companies, you are free to focus all your time and resources on what you do best. If you have chosen your partners for what they do best,

---

[4] Jerry Useem, "Company Goes Crazy Over Partnerships, Gets Committed," *Inc.,* June, 1997.

then you have increased the level of quality in the whole process beyond what you could have achieved on your own. Furthermore, if you have joined forces with substantial companies in your industry, you will find that your company has more clout because you benefit from the "halo effect" of your partners. Consequently, you can bid more successfully against large companies, and you can buy in volume.

On the other hand, strategic alliances suffer from the same problems that plague any partnership. If the partners are not compatible in their business philosophy or corporate culture, there will be constant friction when expectations are not met. When you depend on partners that have a lot of other customers, you have to understand that you may not be their first priority, so you may not be able to get them to respond as quickly as you would like. Moreover, it is difficult for any business owner to give up some control of her operations, especially to another company. It may be even more difficult to get your partners to meet your demands for quality, timeliness, and efficiency. But many business owners have found that the benefits of strategic alliances far outweigh the problems.

KEY 12

Develop a sound technology strategy as part of your competitive advantage

---

A nyone who doesn't understand that technology has revolutionized the way we do business must have been living on a remote island. The impact of technology can be felt in the way industries look and act, even breaking down long-established boundaries between industries to create new, more fluid forms. Small, growing business have the same access to technology and can acquire just as much information as their larger counterparts. Today a small, entrepreneurial business can do business on the Internet alongside a behemoth like AT&T and look just as big, and just as professional.

Still, if you ask the average small business owner if he's using technology in his business, he may point to the PC in the corner of the office and say "yes." The reality is, however, that although 75 percent of small business owners claim to use computers in their businesses, most are still using them as expensive typewriters and calculators. Many business owners claim to have websites but, for the most part, they are used only to present static information.

When you ask these same business owners what their competitive advantage is, they typically reply with such phrases as "niche market," "customer relationships," and "unique product." Rarely do you hear about a business owner who is using technology to propel the business ahead of its competitors. Why is that? The answer lies in the fact that most small business owners still see computer technology as an efficiency tool instead of as an investment in the future success of their businesses, and that's a critical mistake.

Studies have shown that the No. 1 reason for business failure is poor management. And technology strategy is most certainly a management issue. Technology has changed our fundamental perceptions about how business should be conducted. We now expect business transactions to have an immediacy they never had before both in the ability to send and receive information and the ability to access information. We now expect a higher standard of appearance because of the availability of desktop publishing, and we expect to be able to conduct business from anywhere in the world.

Technology is no longer an optional expense for small businesses; it has become a strategic investment that helps entrepreneurs run their businesses smarter and leaner. It is a baseline asset that you invest in just as you invest in equipment and employees. Therefore, it is important that your technology investment supports your business goals. Technology only has value when it is connected to a defined business objective.

Before investing in technology, you need to reach a critical decision point about your business model, so you can decide which business systems are necessary to support that model. Knowing how technology can affect your business model and market reach should be a part of that initial decision making process. Use technology:

◆ To speed up product development;

◆ To speed up organizational and operational processes;

◆ To access and manage information;

◆ To access and manage relationships;

◆ To build a network of strategic partners;

◆ And, most important, to survive.

KEY 13

Create a flexible organization that adapts quickly to change

The corporate downsizing that began in the 1980s was often looked at as an attempt by "big business" to increase profits at the expense of employee jobs. What was not clearly seen until much later was that it really was a recognition by those companies that the world had changed. The technology revolution—the downsizing of computers from mainframes to PCs and the subsequent availability of that technology to smaller businesses—signaled a huge change in the business environment. In fact, one MIT professor found a strong correlation between the decrease in the average number of employees in industrial companies and the growth in investment in information technology. Often, smaller companies are more flexible and can change more rapidly to meet the changing demands of the business environment.

Even the way we manage our companies has to adapt to this new dynamic environment. Hierarchical organizational structures have given way to flatter structures with fewer layers—and preferably no layers—between management and employees. These flatter structures can respond more quickly to market changes.

Cook Specialty, a Pennsylvania-based manufacturer of medical diagnostic products, uses manufacturing cells to create flexibility in its company. Manufacturing cells are integrated teams of people and equipment that can be reconfigured at a moment's notice to meet the demands of a particular customer.

A flexible organization allows you to enter and grow in markets dominated by much larger companies. Because your company is small and adaptable, it has a competitive advantage over an enormous company with an entrenched, bureaucratic structure. You can also find a niche in serving some of the needs of larger companies in the industry that are trying to find ways to respond more quickly.

A start-up company has no choice but to be flexible. By its very nature—born into an uncertain environment—it must be in a position to adapt rapidly just to survive. This can actually be an advantage, because not only can it respond more quickly to shifting circumstances, it has the ability to *create* change. Young entrepreneurs like Marc Andressen, who founded Netscape Communications, used their technology savvy to discover new distribution channels for information and products. Moreover, because they created those channels, they had a "first mover" advantage, which enabled them to control those channels before much larger companies recognized the opportunity.

Michael Gross and Randy Warren founded Global Travel International on the premise that there is no way to anticipate the future, so why not build a company that can respond to change and opportunity instantly.[5] Their successful $10-million-a-year business does just that: they use a cadre of independent agents who make the phone ring at their central office by referring friends and relatives. The lessons they learned can help any business. Pay attention to your customers; they will tell you what to do next. Take advantage of free publicity to increase your sales. Prepare your team for rapid growth before it happens by constantly changing the organization.

---

[5] Donna Fenn, "Masters of Improvisation," *Inc.,* February, 1999, p. 83.

The business of America

is business.

Calvin Coolidge, message to Congress

KEY 14

Make the customer a part of every aspect of your business

W ho really pays your employees? For that matter, who actually pays you? Perhaps, you never thought about it, but it's the customer. Without the customer, you have no business, so it is surprising that so many businesses pay mere lip service to the customer. They claim to provide "customer service," but they only get involved with the customer when they have to.

Today, successful companies have learned to give the customer a real voice in everything the company does, from product development and design, to billing and delivery. They don't just do enough to keep their customers happy; they do more than they have to. They are on a continual hunt for better ways to serve the customer. Charles A. Cocotas knows the value of building long-term relationships with his customers who happen to be dog owners. Understanding that their pets are like children to them, he set out to build a Ritz-Carlton-quality hotel for dogs—Best Friends Pet Resorts and Salons in Connecticut—

where the dogs can take a vacation while their owners do so as well. The owners even have access to a centralized registration system to choose their dog's room and amenities, and to receive updates on their pets.

Building long-term relationships with your customers takes time and dedication, and it will change the way you do business. Many business owners collect information on their customers, but then what do they do with it? Have they collected very personalized information that will allow them to build a relationship? If you only ask customers where and how they bought your product, you never learn how they would really like to purchase your product. And that is far more important information. You may find that they would prefer to purchase your product online for convenience and speed. That is an important piece of information because serving your customers online is less costly than setting up a physical retail outlet, for example.

If you want to make the customer a part of every aspect of your business, you need to ask yourself a few penetrating questions:

◆ Are you willing to put your money where your mouth is and allocate some of your financial resources to customer satisfaction?

◆ Are you willing to forego short-terms gains to gain long-term customer satisfaction?

◆ Are you able to terminate an employee who is not adhering to the pro-customer values of the company?

◆ Will you discuss the customer first at every meeting?

◆ As the owner of the company, are you willing to spend an enormous amount of time with the customer?

If you can answer these questions in the affirmative, then you are ready to begin making the customer the center of your business. When you do that, you will find that you spend far less money trying to recruit new customers because you retain the customers you have and find new ways to serve them.

KEY 15

Hire employees who fit the culture of the company

Ask any business owner what the biggest challenge she faces is, and she will probably answer: *hiring and keeping good people.* Unless your company is in financial trouble and you need more money just to survive, your priority should be identifying and recruiting the best people. Employees, after all, are typically a business owner's biggest expense. Furthermore, once you have hired them, it's difficult to fire them, so it's critically important to spend more time on the front end making sure you get it right.

As you learned in Key 3, your company has a culture that is the result of its core values and beliefs about the way business should be conducted. To maintain that culture, you need to find people who share the same core values and fit seamlessly into your business. Recruiting is not an easy task; but, surprisingly, it's the task that is done least well by most businesses. The mistake most business owners make is that they hire a person for a job; in other words, they hire the person for their job skills alone. Instead, they should be hiring for attitude, self-motivation, communication skills, and personality. After all, your employees spend a substantial portion of their daily lives together. Doesn't it stand to reason that they will perform better if they share a common bond?

You can take several approaches to finding good employees: advertising in local newspapers, recruiting at schools, consulting with

Business is the salt of life.

Thomas Fuller, Gnomologia

employment agencies, and using temporary help services. These are effective and traditional ways to find people. But how do you really find great people? The two best methods are relying on referrals from current employees and others in the industry, and networking at local organizations.

You find your best customers through referrals. Why not try to land employees that way as well. Let your current employees know what you're looking for. They understand the culture of the company, so they're not likely to recommend someone who just wouldn't fit in. Also, make others in your industry aware of your needs. Often your suppliers, distributors, and even customers can refer you to people they think will do a good job for you. They are not likely to recommend someone who will reflect badly on them.

Business owners ignore an important source of information and people when they don't participate in local organizations set up to bring business people together, such as the Chamber of Commerce, the Young Presidents Organization and Rotary International. At meetings of these organizations, you can share your needs and receive the willing help of your business colleagues in finding the best people for your business.

Working with a human resource consultant to set up a recruiting and hiring process is probably money well spent. Human resource consultants can give you invaluable suggestions and make sure that everything you do is within the bounds of labor law. Successfully recruiting and hiring great employees is worth its weight in gold because employees are your most important company asset.

KEY 16

Use an advisory board to guide your growth

When two key employees suddenly left without explanation and six boxes of glass display cases for new stores arrived damaged, Nancy Olsen, founder of Impostors Copy Jewels, was faced with one of those moments that business owners dread. She was in serious financial trouble. Where could she turn? Fortunately, Olsen had recently put together an advisory board for her rapidly growing business, and it was to two of its members that she turned for help. One board member, who was the president of a financial services firm, became her temporary chief financial officer. Another created a new ad campaign for her.[6]

Don Beaver and Don Stapelfeld used their advisory board in a different way. The founders of the New Pig Corporation, a Pennsylvania company that manufactures devices to clean up factory waste, turned to their advisory board to mediate a

[6]Elizabeth Conlin, "Unlimited Partners," *Inc.*, April 1990, p. 71.

disagreement about the way they were going to raise money for the company.

Most companies at one time or another have to look outside their own employees to seek the expert advice they need. An advisory board is a way to create an informal panel of experts that you can tap as needed. Some entrepreneurs resist using outside advisors because they feel they may be giving up some control of their company. The reality is that they are not. In a privately held company, both the formal board of directors and the more informal board of advisors serve at the pleasure of the entrepreneur. As a point of reference, a formal board of directors is required when your company is a corporation and the board of directors selects and hires senior management in addition to preparing the strategic plan for the company. Directors are paid for their positions, so many entrepreneurial companies keep their formal board comprised of inside members and use an advisory board, which is typically unpaid, to get more objective opinions and advice.

Another reason entrepreneurs often don't bother with an advisory board is that they mistakenly believe that someone from the outside could not possibly understand the business. But without an outside advisory board, entrepreneurs risk developing tunnel vision, not thinking out of the box.[7] A diverse advisory board can breathe new life into a floundering company or help the entrepreneur develop a vision for the future of the company.

In creating a board, it makes sense to try to attract professionals like attorneys, accountants and bankers, as well as consultants, presidents of other

[7]Kathleen R. Allen, *Launching New Ventures,* 2nd Ed. Boston: Houghton Mifflin Company, 1999.

companies and for that matter just about anybody with expertise in some area of business, or with valuable contacts, or both.

Putting together an effective advisory board takes thought. It should not be done casually without considering the ramifications. Board members should have similar goals for the company in a broad sense but not be clones of one another. Remember that using friends or family members can be fraught with problems. They may not be able to provide you with the objectivity you need to make decisions, and they may be difficult to remove from the board once they're entrenched.

KEY 17

Recognize when a growth strategy is in trouble

Any growth strategy, no matter how carefully conceived, can run into trouble. While it's not possible to foresee all the things that can go wrong, there are some important "red flags" to watch out for that signal your business may be falling into an unhealthy condition.

Let's first consider management problems. Entrepreneurs often take on significant debt to finance their company's growth. Unfortunately, should anything change, from economic conditions to sales volume to the ability to get supplies, a business that is highly leveraged will have a difficult time meeting its debt obligations. If a business owner finds himself or herself in this situation, it is important to contact creditors immediately to request extended terms. Creditors will often see this as a positive effort to protect them from a possible bankruptcy. Other management problems include:

◆ Poor communications with advisors;

- A dearth of financial reports, which may signal that the owner is not analyzing key issues in the business;

- A lack of financial controls;

- The failure of profits to keep pace with sales growth.

Inventory problems are another contributor to an unhealthy business. If the company does not keep up-to-date inventory records, undervalues its inventory, and has outdated inventory, it is potentially in serious trouble. If you determine that the rate of growth of your inventory outpaces the rate of growth of sales, then you need to take stock of your methods for turning over inventory more quickly via mark downs or for ordering inventory by creating a more just-in-time approach to inventory purchases.

One Maryland electrical contractor discovered too late that he was not monitoring his costs well. While he was able to increase sales by winning several very lucrative bids, his costs ended up being so high that his profit margins declined. By the time he figured out what was wrong, it was too late, and the company collapsed. Even a very simple business can hide some very complex costs that can make or break a company. Ken Woods is the co-owner of Gotta Java, a drive-through coffee outlet in Pasadena, California. To make sure that he understood the costs related to his business, he researched everything from coffee beans to a logo for the business for a period of about three years before he actually opened the business. That kind of dedication to understanding the business gave him the boost he needed to become a success.

Every business experiences some unexpected problems with growth. You can minimize them—

and prevent the excitement of starting a business from turning into a nightmare—by doing your homework. Growth is a positive experience when you plan for it. It means that you have proven the viability of your business concept. The marketplace has accepted your business.

A man's success in business today turns upon the power of getting people to believe he has something they want.

Gerald Stanley Lee, Crowds

KEY 18

It takes money to grow

The old saying, "It takes money to make money," is certainly true when your business starts to grow. Growth is costly both in time and money and often the business isn't throwing off enough extra cash to finance major growth plans and still keep everything else going. The good news is, however, that at this stage of your business, you have many more options for raising money than you did at start-up. Nevertheless, it is important that you understand what it takes to raise growth capital so that you won't let your hopes get unreasonably high.

There are three things to know about raising capital. First, it will always take at least twice as long as you thought it would to accomplish. There is no particular reason for this other than the fact that no one is as anxious to give you money as you are to get it. You should expect to spend several months finding the financing source, then wait several months more while that source does its due diligence and agrees to fund your business, and then spend up to about six months waiting for the check to arrive. The bottom line is: Don't wait until you need the money to begin looking for it.

Second, be prepared for rejection even from a financial source that works with you for months. In fact, the prospect of such rejection makes it critically important for you to look for a backup source even as you are negotiating with the primary source.

Third, you need to be prepared for the cost of raising capital. Upfront costs include the preparation of a business plan and financial statements and perhaps a prospectus or offering document if you are raising equity capital. You will have legal fees, accounting fees, and registration fees in addition to the costs related to printing and mailing documents. These upfront costs must by paid by the entrepreneur prior to receiving any financing.

If you are raising money via a public offering of stock, you will also have "back-end" costs that include an investment banker, legal fees, marketing costs, brokerage fees, and fees charged by federal and state agencies. The total costs can go as high as 25 percent of the offering amount. Some of these costs will be paid out of the proceeds of the offering, but many of them must be paid for in advance of receiving the proceeds.

You can choose from two broad categories of financing: equity and debt. Equity is essentially giving an ownership share in your business to someone who puts his or her capital at risk with no guaranteed return and no protection against loss. Sources of equity funding include personal acquaintances; private investors acting either individually, as "angels," or as participants in a private offering, and venture capitalists.

When you choose a debt instrument to finance your growth, you must provide a business or personal asset as collateral against a loan for which you pay interest. Some of the assets you can use as collateral include equipment, inventory, real estate, or your house or car.

Entrepreneurs typically use a combination of debt and equity to fund their growing businesses. The important thing to remember, however, is that you need to plan for growth by having enough capital on hand to pay the costs of raising growth capital.

KEY 19

A global orientation should be part of your overall growth strategy

When you consider that 95 percent of the world's population and two-thirds of its purchasing power lie outside the United States, it's no surprise that American businesses today are looking to overseas markets to expand. Certainly, with technology and the Internet making it as easy as a mouse click to reach another country, virtually any business can tap into these markets.

There are some very positive reasons to become more aware of the global market and the impact it may have on your growing business. Stretching beyond the boundaries of the United States means that you are not dependent on the American economy or on seasonality in sales in your industry. You are essentially spreading your risk. It may be possible to increase the life of your product by approaching international markets that do not yet offer what you are doing. Furthermore, by using foreign suppliers and manufacturing capability, you may be able to lower your production costs.

It's also important to recognize that even if your company does not want to do business internationally, international businesses may want to do business in your markets in the United States. Consequently, you can't bury your head in the sand. You need to be prepared for global competition, even in your own backyard.

When Domino's decided to enter the Japanese market, it was going where no pizza company had previously succeeded. Domino's knew that providing free delivery, its competitive advantage in the United States, meant nothing to the Japanese, who expected it as a standard service. Therefore, Domino's took a different strategy, downsizing their pizzas to satisfy the smaller appetites of the Japanese and creating much more exciting packaging and brochures to satisfy the Japanese love for gifts. Today, Domino's stores do twice the volume in Japan that they do in the U.S.[8]

The biggest question for most businesses is not *if* they should go global, but *when*. And it's not just about taking your current products abroad. It's about finding new markets and niches for buying and selling opportunities. Before entering the market of another country, you need to understand the nature of the culture in that part of the world. Douglas Lamont, a specialist in international markets, suggests doing research in four basic areas:[9]

1 Who uses the type of product you are planning to sell? How are the users in the foreign country similar or different

---

[8]Kathleen R. Allen, *Launching New Ventures,* 2nd Ed. Boston: Houghton Mifflin Company, 1999.

[9]Douglas F. Lamont, *Global Marketing,* Cambridge, MA: Blackwell Publishers, 1996.

from domestic users? Will this product fit well in the culture of that country?

2 How do people in that country perceive value? What is most important to them— time, quality, service, price? Will you have to change your product to better fit these perceived values?

3 How will you know when a market is changing? Are people in that country ready to accept new ideas? Are they steeped in their own traditions?

4 How can your company establish brand identity and gain market share? Do you have serious competitors in the country? Will customers shift loyalty easily?

For most businesses, the time to go global is after you have established yourself in the domestic market, have attained a significant level of positive cash flow, and have good systems and controls in place.

Far too many corporations
think they have a smart
system and stupid workers.
They've got it backwards.

Bruce E. Babbit,
Lawrence Journal-World

KEY 20

Get onto the Internet to find new customers and retain old ones

For those who thought the Internet was a passing fad (and some pretty important technology people thought that), it's time to join the over 35 percent of the population who use the Internet on a regular basis. The business models are still evolving, so you might still find one that makes you an enormous success. However, remember, we are still in the early adopter stage, and that means it will be an expensive distribution channel if you don't generate the volume you expect. At the present time, most Internet businesses derive their revenues from advertisers on their sites rather than from customers for their products. Other businesses use the Internet as a marketing tool to create customer awareness; still others use it to provide a source of information for their customers and partners.

Although the Internet has been "in business" for a number of years, it is still a place without a lot of rules. What works for one company may not work for another. Nevertheless, putting your business on

Let all your things have their places; let each part of your business have its time.

Benjamin Franklin, Autobiography

the Internet is a way to find out who your customers are and where they are. The easiest and least expensive way to get your company known is to start with forums where users ask and answer questions. For example, AOL has a successful travel forum. One company, Rail Pass Express of Columbus, Ohio, got off the ground by posting information about European train excursions and mentioning in passing that they sell tickets. They also signed their postings with their company name. This was a way to establish their reputation with the forum users. One year later they were able to set up their own web site with online revenues of $300,000.[10]

Starting an e-mail newsletter in another way to begin to gain a presence on the Internet before

---

[10]Kathleen R. Allen, _Growing and Managing an Entrepreneurial Business_, Boston: Houghton Mifflin Company, 1999.

you actually have a site. Newletters full of inter-esting articles and tips will create loyal customers. They are also a great way to retain customers by continually giving them something new. The goal is to get customers coming back to and thinking of your company as a one-stop source in whatever market you are focusing.

The biggest problem for most Internet businesses is getting noticed by potential customers. There are literally millions of websites on the Internet, and while search engines like Yahoo and Excite can help make some sense of this huge mass of businesses, you should not rely on them to guide your potential customers to you. Instead, you will have to do two things to attract customers:

1. Do offline advertising and promotion of your website. Put your web address on your business card and every other piece of promotional material you produce.

2. Link your site with other compatible sites. For example, a travel company could link with a resort so that customers who find the resort site can go directly to the travel site to make arrangements, and vice versa.

A website should be viewed as one more link with the customer. Like your products and services, the site should be perceived as valuable to the cus-tomer and provide benefits they couldn't get by going somewhere else.

KEY 21

Think total quality in every area of your business

In the 1980s, the buzzword was total quality management (T.Q.M.) and it became the mother of a whole series of fads related to the management of organizations. Most of them have gone by the wayside, but T.Q.M. has survived because it has finally come into its own. Businesses finally understand it. T.Q.M. is simply the application of the highest levels of quality throughout your entire organization—in everything you do. The reason that T.Q.M. failed to take hold in the 1980s is that most of the large corporations that attempted to implement it did so in a piecemeal fashion instead of across all the functions of the organization. Today we know that you cannot apply quality measures to only certain parts of your business. You must apply them uniformly across the entire business, because any business is really an integrated system. What you change in one area will affect every other area in some way.

Probably the most successful practitioner of T.Q.M. is Bill Creech, the four-star general who implemented T.Q.M. in the Tactical Air Command during the Gulf War.[11] General Creech thinks of T.Q.M. as five pillars:

1 Commitment by everyone in the organization to the process of T.Q.M.

2 The product, which is what gives the organization focus. Everyone in the company, from the production manager to the bookkeeper produces a product that affects the customer in some way, so quality begins here.

3 The process by which the products of the organization are produced integrates all the areas of the business and has an important impact on the overall quality of the organization.

4 The entire organization, including every employee, must be focused on quality, and it will do this through a decentralized structure that is flexible and supportive.

5 Leadership determines the success of the organization because the leader, the business owner, embodies the spirit, energy, and vision for the company. It's the leader's job to keep the company on track.

There is one more component to be added to Creech's five pillars, and that is the customer. If commitment is the foundation on which all the other pillars rest, then the customer is the roof that unifies the company and holds it together.[12]

---

[11]Bill Creech, *The Five Pillars of TQM*, New York: Truman Talley Books/Plume, 1994.

[12]Kathleen R. Allen, *Growing and Managing an Entrepreneurial Business*, Boston: Houghton Mifflin Company, 1999, p. 187

What managers decide to stop doing is often more important than what they decide to do.

Peter F. Drucker, **New York Times**

Certainly, the commitment of everyone to satisfying the customer brings all the resources of the organization to bear on that single, overriding goal. That is how total quality is achieved.

To infuse total quality management into your business, you need to begin by identifying all the processes in your business, from product development to manufacturing to delivery to billing. Every business is different, but all businesses are comprised of a variety of processes. Once you have these developed, you can then apply a series of questions that will help you arrive at a way to improve quality.

◆ What problem are we having with this process?

- ◆ Where are we now?

- ◆ What are the root causes of the problem we're experiencing?

- ◆ What do we need to do to improve the process?

- ◆ After the improvement has been implemented, ask what happened from our improvement actions?

- ◆ How can we sustain this improvement?

- ◆ What do we need to do next?

This simple question/answer process is an effective way to begin to apply total quality management uniformly across the entire organization and maintain it for the long term.

KEY 22

To go public or not to go public: it's not an easy question to answer

In the world of business, nothing beats an initial public offering for excitement and a sense of absolute power. Certainly today, with Internet start-ups like Geocities.com and Amazon.com attracting millions of dollars of investment capital and reaching billions of dollars in market valuation, the rush to do an I.P.O. is on. For some lucky entrepreneurs, it has been the greatest adventure of their lives; but for others, going public was an enormous mistake, if not an absolute disaster.

In 1996, Smed International, an office-furnishings maker based in Calgary, Alberta, Canada, went public and raised $42 million in one day. Four months later, however, the stock dropped from $20 a share to $5 a share, due largely to the Asian financial crisis and plummeting international sales. In the wake of a layoff of 350 employees, investors were angry, and suddenly the $42 million Smed had raised became a tremendous burden. This example reflects perhaps the biggest negative of becoming a public company. You are now responsible first to your shareholders, and your personal goals for the company come second.

Because the Securities and Exchange Commission, or S.E.C., has made it easier and less costly for smaller companies to go public, more of them are doing it. It is an enormous source of interest-free capital to fund growth and expansion, pay off debt or do product development. A public company has more prestige and clout in the industry, and it's easier to raise money through a secondary offering or by borrowing against the stock. A public company also has an easier time attracting top employees because it can offer them stock options.

Still, there are some disadvantages that business owners should carefully consider. Statistics on the success rate of public companies are sobering. In the 1980s, 3,186 firms went public; only 58 percent of them are still listed on one of the many stock exchanges. Furthermore, only one-third of these firms had stock values above their issue price.[13]

Going public is an expensive process, often running well over $300,000, a figure that does not include a 7 percent to 10 percent commission to the underwriter. It is also a time-consuming process. Many chief executives report that they spent most of every week over four to six months preparing for the stock offering.

Once the company is public, everything that company does becomes public information, including its annual financial reports. It also has significant reporting requirements to the S.E.C. Lastly, a public company is under extreme pressure to perform in the short term to satisfy its investors with

---

[13]Gary D. Zeune, "Ducks in a Row: Orchestrating the Flawless Stock Offering," *Corporate Cash-flow*, February, 1993.

healthy dividends. The pressure to show immediate gains may prevent the company from
achieving its long-term goals.

Going public is a serious decision with serious
consequences. Any business owner contemplating
such a strategy should seek out advice from those
who have done it and weigh the pros and cons
carefully. If retaining your corporate culture and
long-term goals is important to you, you may
decide to seek private investor capital instead.

KEY 23

Find an angel to give the company a jump-start on growth

L et's face it. Approximately 99 percent of all businesses do not attract professional venture capital. For all the press and hype, the truth is that only very particular types of businesses attract venture capital. These are ventures that can provide extraordinarily high returns in a period of three to five years and are most often found in the high-tech and biotechnology areas. This is not a bad thing, because entrepreneurs will have to give up a lot to take on the types of institutional investors that populate the venture-capital pools.

A more realistic and entrepreneurial alternative is to find a so-called angel. Angels are part of what is called the informal-risk capital market, which happens to be the largest pool of capital in the U.S., more than $50 billion. It would seem that as powerful as angels are, it would not be difficult to find them; but it is. They do not advertise by traditional means, and you can't find them in traditional ways. You find angels or private investors through a process known as networking, participating in community organizations and letting your key professional advisors—bankers, accountants, attorneys—know what you need. This process takes time, so it's important to start networking to find an angel long before you actually need the capital.

Private investors don't all look alike, but they do have several common characteristics. They are usually educated males in their 40s or 50s who have been successful entrepreneurs themselves. They normally invest near to their homes in amounts that generally range from $10,000 to $500,000 or more. They're looking for early-stage ventures and they tend to prefer manufacturing, high technology, energy and resources, and service businesses. Retail ventures and restaurants are less likely investment targets because of their high failure rate. Private investors enjoy being part of a rapidly growing business, so they will often stay with the investment for a much longer period of time than a venture capitalist. To the benefit of the entrepreneur, they usually make decisions quickly and their requirements and due diligence are not as stringent.

You can find private investors in some very unexpected places. For example, Ivan Makil, president of the Salt River Pima-Maricopa Indian community in Scottsdale, Arizona, manages a pool of investment capital focusing on businesses that meet the tribe's vision and goals and that are environmentally sensitive.

Private investors often prefer a deal that is structured with convertible preferred stock. This means that their stock will convert to common stock with voting rights if the company goes public. Alternatively, they can sell the stock back to the company at the end of a specified period. Other investors prefer convertible debentures, a debt instrument that allows the investor to receive interest payments and then the option of converting the principal to stock after a defined period of time.

Private investors are a good source for both start-up and growth capital. They're easy to deal with because they've usually been entrepreneurs and understand what you're going through. The important thing is to start networking right away so you'll have someone in mind when you need capital.

Business is other

peoples money.

Madame De Girardin, **Marguerite**

KEY 24

Make your company a learning organization

The concept of change has been stressed throughout this book. The countries of the world really are closer, things do happen more quickly, and information is more readily available to anyone because of technology. Most businesses are no longer operating in stable environments where they don't often have to change. Successful companies today are in continual flux.

To prosper in this environment, your organization must put itself in a learning mode, developing a system for constantly seeking out new information and applying it to the company. Peter Senge, in his best-selling book *The Fifth Discipline*, asserts that the superior organization of the future will be one that encourages learning at every level—individual, team, department, organization.[14]

---

[14]Peter Senge, *The Fifth Discipline: The Art and Practice of the Learning Organization,* New York: Currency/Doubleday, 1990.

A learning organization is not solely focused on gathering information. That is only part of the picture. More important, it is focused on constantly renewing itself at both the organizational and individual levels. This renewal comes about in five ways.

Setting individual goals. Every individual in the organization has the responsibility of setting improvement goals for herself. Maybe it's to learn to speak in front of an audience or learn a new software program. In whatever way the employee wants to improve herself, it is management's responsibility to facilitate her ability to do that and encourage her through training, incentives, and support.

Finding congruence with perceived realities. Everyone looks at the world differently based on his own experiences and background. When you bring many people into an organization with many different views on how things should work, you often have clashes. Management needs to provide a safe environment where individuals can explore their differing perceptions and learn to communicate better.

Sharing a common vision. Recall from Key 3 that vision is an important ingredient to successful growth. Vision is not an edict that comes from the top down. It is rather a force that pulls everyone together to take the company in one direction. The product-development team of one technology company was forced to develop a new computer at a time when the company was facing a crisis. At one point in the product-development process, the engineers learned that critical software was far behind schedule. Determined to save their company at the expense of their own

> So much of what we call management consists in making it difficult for people to work.

Peter Drucker

time and health, the engineers spent an entire night working on the problem and completed two to three months of effort in one night. This type of effort is an example of commitment to a shared vision.

Learning at the team level. Organizations learn at the team level when individuals are able to get beyond their personal perceptions and beliefs and align themselves with a single purpose and goal. Successful, learning teams become powerful stakeholders in the company because they always tend to be on the leading edge of knowledge.

Thinking of the organization as a system. Everyone in the company must see the business as a whole system. Employees must be able to see how their actions affect other areas of the business.

Building a learning organization won't happen overnight. It takes time, but it is time well spent preparing your business to face change.

KEY 25

Follow a different model for hypergrowth

I f you have a business built on a technology you have developed or licensed, or you have an early-stage Internet company with huge potential, many of the traditional business models don't apply to you. When technology is the product, your company will usually experience a different adoption cycle than most products.

When you introduce your product, particularly if it is one that will revolutionize the market, the first purchasers will be what are called "early adopters." Early adopters are people who are constantly searching for new technology and want to be the first to own it. They often do what technology developers call a *beta test* on new technology to look for any bugs before it goes to the mass market. This is a critical time in the life of a new technology because between early adoption and mass market acceptance is what Geoffrey Moore has termed the "chasm". The chasm is that period when the mainstream market is still not comfortable with the technology and is waiting to see how things shake out.[15] If the product satisfies the early adopters and they spread the word, it is possible that the marketplace will begin to shift *en masse* from the old technology to the new in what is termed a *flash point*. Once the business has successfully crossed the chasm, it begins to seek out niche markets. The goal is to claim as many niches as possible to build up critical mass and momentum for the technology. It is the pent-up demand for the new technology that then sends the business into hypergrowth.

Although the most common place to find hypergrowth is computer technology in the Silicon Valley of California, hypergrowth can also be seen in other industries like pharmeceuticals, broadcasting, aerospace, and others. Mr. Moore has called the period when the business is in hypergrowth "the tornado." Inside the tornado, things happen very fast, and a business that is not prepared can actually reverse the growth trend, discourage customers whose demand is not being met, and open itself to being overtaken by a competitor.

There are many important lessons to be learned about the nature of hypergrowth.

◆ To be successful, you must be willing to attack your competition ruthlessly. You are trying to make your technology a standard in a competitive industry, and there is no other way to do it.

◆ You will need to expand the distribution channel as quickly as possible even at the expense of the customer in the short term. Demand is there; you need to provide the

---

[15]Geoffrey A. Moore, *Inside the Tornado*, New York: HarperCollins Publishers, Inc., 1995.

supply. You should expand to as many distribution channels as possible. The price of the technology will come down rapidly, so it's important to increase volume.

◆ Focus on the process above anything else. You need to be able to ship quickly and reliably and stay on top of problems.

◆ Drive to the next lower price point. If you are first to hit the next lower price point, you pick up a whole new market segment. If you don't decrease prices at the appropriate time, you risk losing your customers to clones.

Perhaps most important, have good, reliable partners in place before you reach hypergrowth. You will have to depend on them for your very existence.

Do business, but be

not a slave to it.

Thomas Fuller, Gnomologia

REFERENCES

Allen, Kathleen R., *Growing and Managing an Entrepreneurial Business*, Boston: Houghton Mifflin Company, 1999.

Allen, Kathleen R., *Launching New Ventures*, 2nd, Ed. Boston: Houghton Mifflin Company, 1999.

Collins, Jim and Jerry I. Porras (199). *Built to Last, Successful Habits of Visionary Companies*, New York: Harper Business, 1994.

Conlin, Elizabeth, "Unlimited Partners," *Inc.,* April 1990, p. 71.

Creech, Bill, *The Five Pillars of TQM*, New York: Truman Talley Books/Plume, 1994.

Greco, Susan, "Share the Power," *Inc.,* February, 1999, p. 52.

Lamont, Douglas F., *Global Marketing*, Cambridge, MA: Blackwell Publishers, 1996.

Moore, Geoffrey A., *Inside the Tornado*, New York: HarperCollins Publishers, Inc., 1995.

Senge, Peter, *The Fifth Discipline: The Art and Practice of the Learning Organization*, New York: Currency/Doubleday, 1990.

Useem, Jerry, "Company Goes Crazy Over Partnerships, Gets Committed," *Inc.,* June 1997.

Zeune, Gary D., "Ducks in a Row: Orchestrating the Flawless Stock Offering," *Corporate Cashflow*, February, 1993.

INDEX

AUTHOR

KATHLEEN R. ALLEN, Ph.D., is a Professor of Entrepreneurship at The Lloyd Greif Center for Entrepreneurial Studies at the Marshall School of the University of Southern California. She has written two widely-adopted books on entrepreneurship—*Entrepreneurship and Small Business Management* and *Launching New Ventures: An Entrepreneurial Approach*—and most recently *Growing and Managing an Entrepreneurial Business* and *Tips and Traps for Entrepreneurs*. She is a frequent contributor to *Inc.* magazine, *The New York Times*, *The Los Angeles Times*, and *Los Angeles Business Journal*, and is the cofounder and Executive Vice President/CFO of Gentech Corporation, a technology-based manufacturing company.